'Spice Up
Your Speech!'

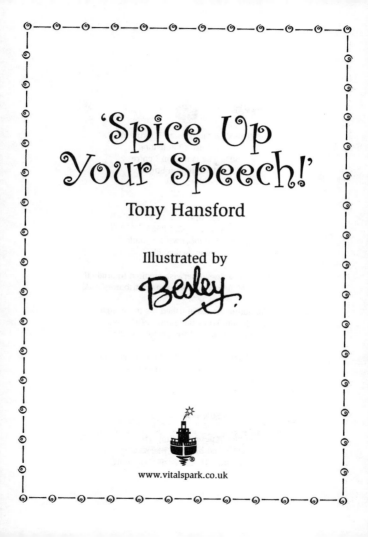

'Spice Up Your Speech!'

Tony Hansford

Illustrated by

Besley

www.vitalspark.co.uk

The Vital Spark is an imprint of
Neil Wilson Publishing
303a The Pentagon Centre
36 Washington Street
GLASGOW
G3 8AZ

Tel: 0141-221-1117
Fax: 0141-221-5363
E-mail: info@nwp.sol.co.uk
www.nwp.co.uk

A catalogue record for this book is available
from the British Library.

1   3   5   7   9   10   8   6   4   2

ISBN 1-903238-53-6

Typeset in Slimbach
Designed by Mark Blackadder
Printed by Omnia Books, Glasgow

Contents

Introduction

We all envy those brilliant speakers we see on TV chat shows and quiz games, at dinners and social events. How easy they seem to make it and how witty their impromptu remarks can be. If you're like me you always think of that brilliant riposte the next day – if at all.

In truth 99 per cent of the speakers we admire rely on good preparation for those seemingly 'spontaneous' remarks. They also have impeccable timing. A remark made out of context will have very little effect, but if made on the right occasion and timed correctly it can create a terrific impression.

I spent 34 years searching for the odd joke, comment or one-liner that could be used to liven up a presentation or speech – or just to use in the bar with colleagues. Over this time I have compiled a notebook of amusing things. After many friends had approached me, asking for some of these stories when they were preparing a talk or a speech I decided the time had come for my collection to become a book.

'Spice Up Your Speech!' is a condensed source of quotes, sayings, and one-liners that you can dip into for inspiration when you have to make a speech or presentation at a business or social event. Or perhaps when you are just going out with friends and want one or two easily remembered stories to raise a laugh. Material used from this book should be delivered with discretion and deference to the company you are in.

Speeches, talks or presentations are a bit like meals – they can be bland or they can be a real treat, they have to be planned and the ingredients carefully selected. I hope this book will provide some of the spices or seasonings to add that little extra something to your speech and provide some light relief.

Tony Hansford
April 2002

1.
Age

He's in God's waiting room.

He's in the prime of his senility.

You can't rest on your laurels – they turn into wreaths.

Two old school friends met aged 76:
'How are you?'
'Great.'
'Keeping regular?'
'Yes, seven o'clock every morning.'
'Why, that's great.'
'Not so great, I don't get up till eight.'

(George Burns)

A very old man likes going out with young girls.
His friend asks him one day, 'Why don't you go out with girls of your own age?'
He answers, 'There aren't any girls of my age.'

(George Burns)

9

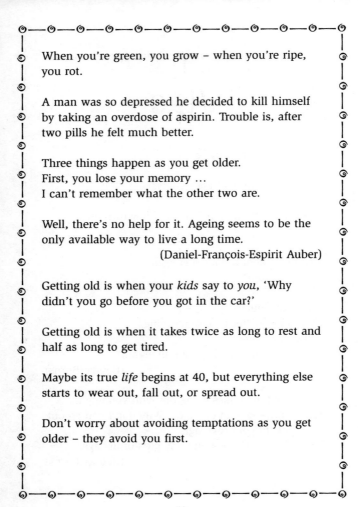

When you're green, you grow – when you're ripe, you rot.

A man was so depressed he decided to kill himself by taking an overdose of aspirin. Trouble is, after two pills he felt much better.

Three things happen as you get older.
First, you lose your memory …
I can't remember what the other two are.

Well, there's no help for it. Ageing seems to be the only available way to live a long time.
(Daniel-François-Espirit Auber)

Getting old is when your *kids* say to *you*, 'Why didn't you go before you got in the car?'

Getting old is when it takes twice as long to rest and half as long to get tired.

Maybe its true *life* begins at 40, but everything else starts to wear out, fall out, or spread out.

Don't worry about avoiding temptations as you get older – they avoid you first.

Growing old isn't so bad when you consider the alternative.

Although he's 60 years old, in bed he's like an animal. He sleeps all through the winter.

He said that if he'd known he was going to live that long, he would have looked after himself better.

When my father was 80 and in an old folk's home, a little old lady there had her eye on him. She claimed to have gypsy blood and said, 'I can tell you how old you are and where you're from.' 'How?' He asked. She slipped her hand under his bedsheet, groped around a bit and said, 'You're a Capricorn, still vigorous, married three times, 80 years old, and you were born in Jersey.'
My father replied, 'My God ... you're right! But how on earth can you tell all that by feeling me up?'
'You told me yesterday.'

An old man is someone who can't take 'yes' for an answer.

I lose my temper sometimes because it's the only part of me left to lose.

You're looking at a man with two weeks to live – my wife's gone away for a fortnight.

Life is a malady whose one medicine is death.
(Abu'l-'Alaá Al'Ma'arri)

Old age is a disease you can't look forward to being cured of.

They are all well into heart attack country now, where life's road gets steep and a man is easily winded. Women go on and on but men drop like flies around this age. (Garrison Keillor)

A man of 70 went to his doctor:
'I want you to lower my sex drive.'
Doctor: 'Look, it's all in your mind.'
Patient: 'I know – that's why I want you to lower it.'

His idea of exercise is going to a self-service restaurant.

It's not that I'm afraid to die. I just don't want to be there when it happens. (Woody Allen)

I used to get my leg over – now I can't get it back.

I still chase women – but only when they're going downhill.

Wrinkles are where the smiles have been.

(Mark Twain)

He uses Grecian 2000 – and he looks like a 2000-year-old Grecian.

Experience is something you don't get until just after you need it.

To die will be an awfully big adventure.

(J M Barrie in *Peter Pan*)

To me old age is always 15 years older than I am.

(Bernard Baruch)

When a man's friends begin to compliment him about looking young, he may be sure that they think he is growing old.

(Washington Irving)

You know you're getting older when:

The gleam in your eye is from the sun hitting your bifocals.

You sink your teeth into a steak – and they stay there.

You look forward to a dull evening.

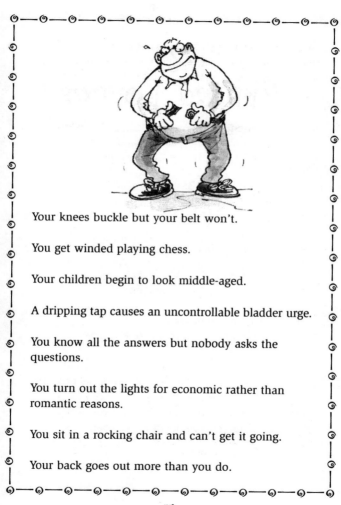

Your knees buckle but your belt won't.

You get winded playing chess.

Your children begin to look middle-aged.

A dripping tap causes an uncontrollable bladder urge.

You know all the answers but nobody asks the questions.

You turn out the lights for economic rather than romantic reasons.

You sit in a rocking chair and can't get it going.

Your back goes out more than you do.

2.
Armed Forces

'Do you want a commission?'
'No thanks, I'd rather have a regular wage.'

It was a good outfit. The men were very proud of their officer – and he was very proud of his privates.

Sergeant to the new recruits: 'To save you walking, I'm going to march you down to the cookhouse.'

Officer: 'We leave at 1500 hours.'
Soldier: 'You'll have to let me know when that is –
my watch only goes up to 12.'   (Spike Milligan)

An officer in a war zone, reviewing newly arrived
Australian troops says to one, 'Hello soldier, did you
come up here to die?'
'No sir, I came with the advance party yesterdie.'

Be silent when you speak to an officer!

Old Soldier: 'My grandfather was killed at Waterloo.'
Young man: 'Oh really – what platform?'

3.
As...

As welcome as a fart in a space suit.

As welcome as a piranha in a bidet.

As welcome as a rattle-snake in a lucky dip.

As broke as the Ten Commandments.

As much use as an out-of-date lottery ticket.

As much use as giving a fish a bath.

As much fun as having a verucca burnt out.

As true as you are a foot high.

As quiet as a mouse pissing on cotton wool.

A man is as old as he feels, and a woman is as old as she looks.

4.
Being Positive

I think I'm more positive now.

The way I see it, if you want a rainbow, you've got to put up with the rain.   (Dolly Parton)

I used to be indecisive, now I'm not so sure.

The lion does not roar in reply to the braying of the ass.

You can't plough a field by turning it over in your mind.

A gorgeous woman goes to tattooist and asks 'Can you tattoo a wildcat on my knee?'
The tattooist replies, 'We're having a sale on giraffes this week.'

'There are no such things as problems, only opportunities!'
'In that case I wonder if you'd give me some help with an insurmountable opportunity.'

I love it when it snows. It's the only time of the year when my garden looks as good as everyone else's.

Pessimism, once you get used to it, is just as agreeable as optimism.

(Arnold Bennett)

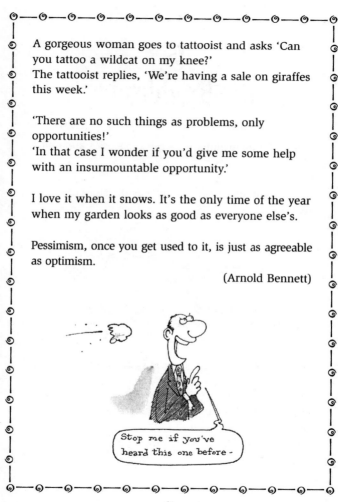

Stop me if you've heard this one before –

5.
Books

I like reading dictionaries – but the stories are a bit short.

He thought an autobiography was the story of a motor car.

The *Penguin Book of Quotations* – I didn't know penguins had so much to say.

Uncle to nephew, 'Would you like a book for your birthday?'

Nephew, 'No thanks, I've already got a book.'

A schoolboy enters a second-hand bookshop and shyly purchases a book entitled *How to Hug*. After hurrying back to his bedroom he discovers he has bought Volume Six of the *Encyclopaedia Brittanica*.

Poetry is the stuff in books that doesn't quite reach the margins.

There are worse crimes than burning books. One of them is not reading them.

(Ioseph Brodsky)

Science Fiction is no more written for scientists than ghost stories are written for ghosts.

(Brian Aldiss)

6.
Career

Whenever a friend succeeds a little something in me dies. (Gore Vidal)

Journalist – organised the 'Spot the ball' competition in the *Sunbathers Weekly*.

Music critic for *Exchange & Mart*.

Bouncer for Mothercare.

Be nice to people on your way up because you'll meet them on your way down.   (Wilson Mizner)

He bought a paper shop but it blew away.

Gardener – used to sprinkle whisky on the grass so it came up half cut.

He got the boot from the shoe shop.

She had a job at the glue factory but couldn't stick it.

She was going to be a doctor but she didn't have the patience.

He's attended lots of courses – Turnberry, Gleneagles, St Mellion.

He had to leave the navy – he got his fingers badly crushed when they called: 'All hands on deck.'

He's been doing the work of two men – Laurel & Hardy.

It's not enough to succeed. Others must fail.

(Gore Vidal)

Her wishbone is where her backbone should be.

I'd like to help you out – which way did you come in?

They're in the iron and steel business – she does the ironing, he does the stealing.

No one on their deathbed ever said, 'I wish I'd spent more time at the office.'

We all know the boss is a meticulous man. He once received a ransom note for his wife – and sent it back to the kidnappers for retyping.

Business is something that you go out of when you don't have any of it.

A reunion is when a lot of people get together to see who's falling apart.

'I applied for a job as a rubbish collector.'
'Any experience?'
'No, I thought I'd pick it up as I went along.'

He speaks two languages – English and rubbish.

I've been on the road so long I find it difficult to sleep in a room that doesn't have a number on the door.

He wasn't a high flier – more of a low flier supported by occasional gusts of wind.

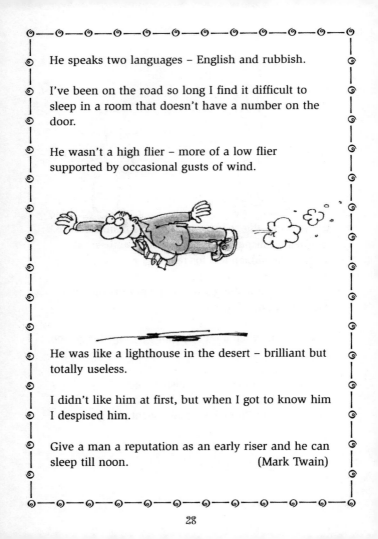

He was like a lighthouse in the desert – brilliant but totally useless.

I didn't like him at first, but when I got to know him I despised him.

Give a man a reputation as an early riser and he can sleep till noon.   (Mark Twain)

I want to make it clear that I've got principles, and if you don't like them – I've got others.

Herr Cutt: the German barber.
His partner: Herr Lakker.

His mind goes on holiday and leaves his mouth in charge.

On being told his 'human canonball' had died the circus owner said: 'I'm very sorry to hear that – men of his calibre are hard to find.'

The clown used to eat watches, but he was told to cut it out, as it was too time consuming.

The important thing about selling is honesty – if you can fake that, you've got it made.

A diplomat is someone who always remembers a woman's birthday – but never her age.

(Robert Frost)

The artist had a one man show, which was a great success – one man turned up.

My indecision is final.

7.
Clothes

Fashion is made to become unfashionable.

(Coco Chanel)

He got a job on the railways – so he turned up in a tracksuit!

The Right Hon was a tubby little chap who looked as if he had been poured into his clothes and had forgotten to say 'When!'.

(P G Wodehouse)

Two little girls were in the school playground.
'I know how to tell how old teacher is.'
'How?'
'Look in her knickers.'
'How does that tell you how old she is?'
'Well, I looked in mine and it's got age 4 to 6.'

Is that a pistol you have in your pocket or are you just pleased to see me?   (Mae West)

Fashion can be bought. Style one must possess.

The glory of God is man, and the glory of man is his dress.

Life nowadays is dominated and complicated by the zip. Blouses zip up, skirts zip down, ski-ing suits zip everywhere ... Why? Is there anything more deadly than a zip that turns nasty on you?

(Agatha Christie)

She fitted into my biggest armchair as if it had been built round her by someone who knew they were wearing armchairs tight about the hips that season.

(P G Wodehouse)

A little of what you call frippery is very necessary towards looking like the rest of the world.

(Abigail Adams)

Fashion, noun, a despot whom the wise ridicule and obey.

(Ambrose Bierce)

High heels were invented by a woman who had been kissed on the forehead.

(Christopher Darlington Morley)

I was the first woman to burn my bra – it took the fire department four days to put it out.

(Dolly Parton)

A dress makes no sense unless it inspires men to want to take it off you. (François Sagan)

To call a fashion wearable is the kiss of death. No new fashion worth its salt is ever wearable.
(Eugenia Sheppard)

Where's the man could ease a heart
Like a satin gown?

(Dorothy Parker)

8. Doctor & Health

Doctor 'I've some good news and some bad news. The bad news is – a change is taking place in your body, your male hormones are decreasing, and you're turning into a woman.'
'Good heavens – what's the good news?'
'I think I love you.'

He went to the doctor with a stiff neck – he'd swallowed his Viagra too quickly.

Patient to sexy nurse:
'Is it true you go all stiff when you die?'
'Yes.'
'Well, I think I've started.'

Man finds a tennis ball and puts it in his pocket. In the pub later the landlord says, pointing at his trousers, 'Gosh, what's that?'
'That's a tennis ball.'
'How horrible, I had that in the elbow. It must be painful.'

People keep telling me I'm deaf but my doctor tells me not to listen to them.

Doctor: 'Strip off ... You'll have to diet.'
'What colour.'

'Doctor, I'm having trouble with this leg, it's a cramp-like pain.'
'It's old age.'
'That's funny, the other leg's the same age and it's perfectly OK.'   (Spike Milligan)

My husband has sinus trouble. He's always saying 'Sign us a cheque for this, sign us a cheque for that.'

Doctor, doctor:–

'People ignore me.'
'Next please.'

'I think I'm a pair of curtains.'
'Pull yourself together.'

'I'm a biscuit'
'A square one with holes in it?'
'Yes.'
'You're crackers.'

'Doctor, doctor, I think I'm a pack of cards.'
'Sit down – I'll deal with you in a minute.'

Doctor, doctor, I keep
thinking I'm a dog.'
'How long have you
felt like this?'
'Ever since I was a
puppy.'

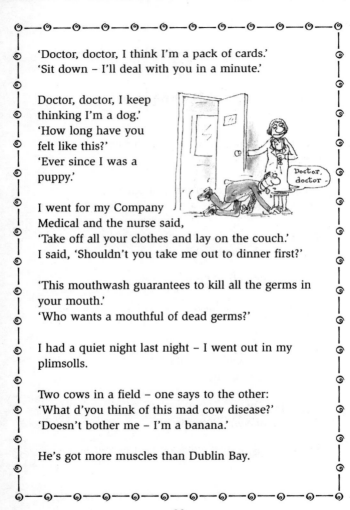

I went for my Company
Medical and the nurse said,
'Take off all your clothes and lay on the couch.'
I said, 'Shouldn't you take me out to dinner first?'

'This mouthwash guarantees to kill all the germs in
your mouth.'
'Who wants a mouthful of dead germs?'

I had a quiet night last night – I went out in my
plimsolls.

Two cows in a field – one says to the other:
'What d'you think of this mad cow disease?'
'Doesn't bother me – I'm a banana.'

He's got more muscles than Dublin Bay.

9. Drink

TITUS ANDRONICUS

I've made it a rule never to drink by daylight and never to refuse a drink after dark.   (H L Mencken)

I don't drink any more – but I don't drink any less either.

I distrust camels and anyone else who can go a week without a drink.   (Joe E Lewis)

I don't drink so much now – I spill most of it.

Twenty-four hours in a day. Twenty-four beers in a case. Coincidence?

I haven't had a drink since 1945!
Congratulations.
Thank you, but I'll probably get one before closing time at 11.00 hours.

The proper union of gin and vermouth is a great and sudden glory; it is one of the happiest marriages on earth, and one of the shortest lived.

(Bernard De Voto)

He lost all his luggage at Heathrow – the cork came out of the bottle.

Liquor is not a necessity. It is a means of momenatarily sidestepping necessity.

(Clifton Fadiman)

My father was 80 and didn't need glasses – he drank straight from the bottle.

The nearest he ever gets to being tidy is drinking his whisky neat.

'Why did you come home half drunk?'
'I ran out of money.'

'This is a very good seven-year-old whisky.'
'It's a bit small for it's age.'

Accuracy is soluble in alcohol.

He's a member of the Ghost Club – they hang
around drinking spirits.

You can no more keep a martini in the refrigerator
than you can keep a kiss there.

(Bernard De Voto)

They were going to ask
him to launch a ship
but were frightened
he wouldn't let
go of the bottle.

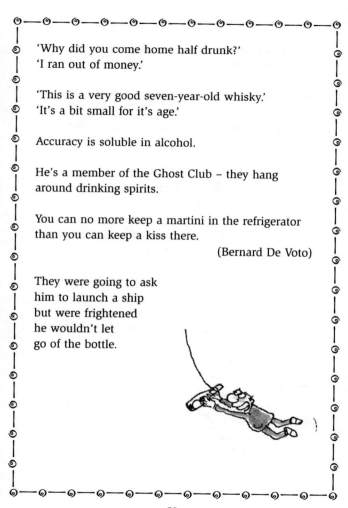

He's read so much about the evils of drink that he's given up reading.

An alcoholic is someone you don't like who drinks as much as you do.

Liquor improves with age – the older you get, the more you like it.

He was standing on a table shouting 'Pour it over me, I can't drink it fast enough.'

He was standing in a sandbucket singing *The Desert Song*.

He's got a drinking problem – he's only got one mouth.

I don't know what he's on but I wouldn't mind half a bottle of it.

Enjoy another glass, for you see what the end is.

Driver to policeman who stopped him 'What did I do wrong officer?'
Policeman 'Nothing – I smelt you as you went by'.

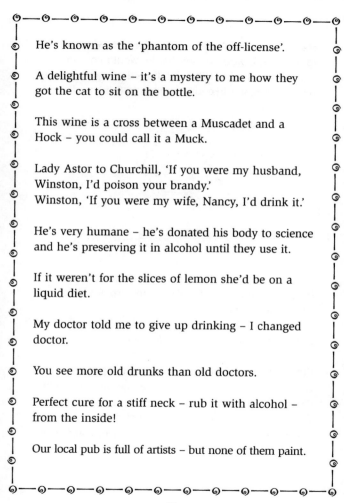

He's known as the 'phantom of the off-license'.

A delightful wine – it's a mystery to me how they got the cat to sit on the bottle.

This wine is a cross between a Muscadet and a Hock – you could call it a Muck.

Lady Astor to Churchill, 'If you were my husband, Winston, I'd poison your brandy.'
Winston, 'If you were my wife, Nancy, I'd drink it.'

He's very humane – he's donated his body to science and he's preserving it in alcohol until they use it.

If it weren't for the slices of lemon she'd be on a liquid diet.

My doctor told me to give up drinking – I changed doctor.

You see more old drunks than old doctors.

Perfect cure for a stiff neck – rub it with alcohol – from the inside!

Our local pub is full of artists – but none of them paint.

John Arlott built up a collection of wine for his retirement. It worried him that he would not put away enough to last him. When he did retire he was worried that he wouldn't live long enough to drink it all.

He's now on a balanced diet – he carries a drink in each hand.

I'm not so think as you drunk I am.

I'm only a beer teetotaler – not a champagne teetotaler.   (George Bernard Shaw)

Work is the curse of the drinking classes.
                                   (Oscar Wilde)

I must get out of these wet clothes and into a dry martini. (Billy Wilder)

Claret is the liquor for boys; port for men: but he who aspires to be a hero must drink brandy.

(Johnson)

Who loves not wine, woman and song,
Remains a fool, his whole life long. (Martin Luther)

We run a tight ship – lately, however, some of us have been getting tight too often.

Drinking when we are not thirsty and making love at any season is all there is to distinguish us from the animals. (Pierre-Augustin de Beaumarshais)

'Your glass is empty, would you like another?'
'Now what would I want with two empty glasses?'

He ruined his health by drinking to other peoples'.

Great fury, like great whisky, requires long fermentation. (Truman Capote)

Two fat blokes in a pub. One says to the other 'Your round.' The other replies 'So are you.'

A Scotsman was asked to define the difference between sufficiency and excess.
'Moderation is my rule, nine or ten is reasonable refreshment, but after that it's apt to degenerate into drinking.'

My favourite whisky is the next one.

He joined Alcoholics Anonymous but it didn't stop him drinking, now he just drinks under a false name.

'Is that Alcoholics Anonymous?'
'Yes it is – do you want to join?'
'No – I want to resign.'

Eight pints of beer and a loud fart are the signs of a free spirit.   (George Melly)

He slept like a log last night – he had his head in the fireplace.

It was in Italy he realised he had a drink problem – the Leaning Tower of Pisa looked straight.

When asked who had the greatest influence on his career, Jimmy Greaves replied, 'Vladimir Smirnoff.'

10.
Food

Waiter, waiter...

A good eater must be a good man; for a good eater must have a good digestion, and a good digestion depends on a good conscience. (Disraeli)

The beef was so rare a good vet could have had it on its feet again.

Life itself is the proper binge. (Julia Child)

Seeing is deceiving. It's eating that's believing.
(James Thurbor)

I like Welshmen but I couldn't eat a whole one.

Dolphins are so intelligent that within a few days of captivity they have trained humans to stand at the side of a pool and throw fish to them.

Waiter: 'Is there anything else I can bring you?'
'Yes please, a very small bill.'

Epitaph for a waiter?
'By and by
God caught his eye.'
(David McCord)

A snackbar in Florida's Everglades – 'Let me have a crocodile sandwich please, and make it snappy.'

People who eat white bread have no dreams.
(Diana Vreeland)

It's such a rough neighbourhood that Tesco puts 'steal by' dates on the food.

We found this Italian restaurant run by the Mafia. Its speciality was broken leg of lamb.

When faced with two eggs – Un oeuf is enough.

Waiter: 'Do you have a reservation?'
Customer: 'Well I'm not sure about the music.'

Cooking is like love. It should be entered into with
abandon or not at all.   (Harriet Van Horne)

Cheese for desert is rather like *Paradise Lost* in that
everyone thinks they *ought* to like it, but still you
don't notice too many people actually curling up
with it.   (Peg Bracken)

She's on a seafood diet – she only has to see food
and she eats it.

You can have your cake and eat it: the only trouble
is you get fat.   (Julian Barnes)

He went to the 'Karate' school of cooking – one of
his chops would kill you.

11.
How and Why

Why is the alphabet in that order?

Why, if white is a virginal colour, do nuns wear black?

Why is there only one Monopolies Commission?

Why do men have nipples?

What is the speed of dark?

What happens if you get scared half to death twice?

Why do kamikaze pilots wear helmets?

How does the person who drives the snowplough get to work?

Why is the sky blue?

How do insects stick to walls?

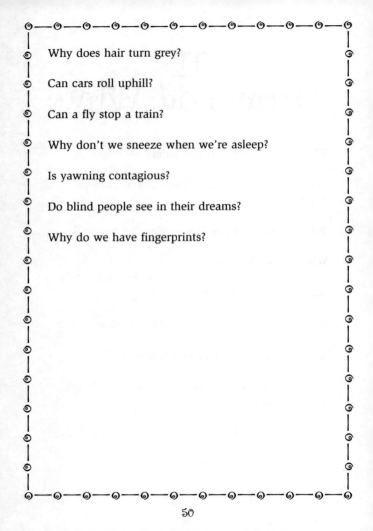

Why does hair turn grey?

Can cars roll uphill?

Can a fly stop a train?

Why don't we sneeze when we're asleep?

Is yawning contagious?

Do blind people see in their dreams?

Why do we have fingerprints?

12.
Love & Marriage

The love that moves the sun and the other stars.

(Dante Alighieri)

If you love something,
Set it free.
If it comes back,
It's yours.
If it doesn't,
It never was.

All mankind love a lover.   (Ralph Emerson)

His wife would divorce him tomorrow if she could find a way to do it without making him happy.

A girl must marry for love, then keep marrying until she finds it.

(Zsa Zsa Gabor)

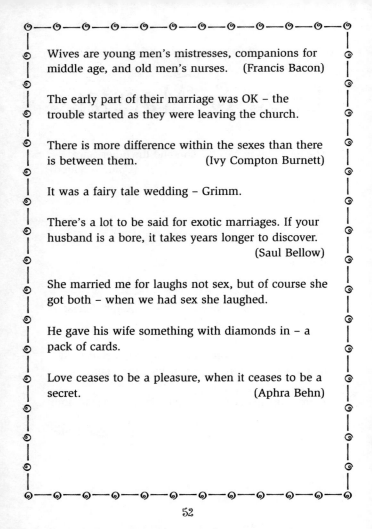

Wives are young men's mistresses, companions for middle age, and old men's nurses.   (Francis Bacon)

The early part of their marriage was OK – the trouble started as they were leaving the church.

There is more difference within the sexes than there is between them.   (Ivy Compton Burnett)

It was a fairy tale wedding – Grimm.

There's a lot to be said for exotic marriages. If your husband is a bore, it takes years longer to discover.
(Saul Bellow)

She married me for laughs not sex, but of course she got both – when we had sex she laughed.

He gave his wife something with diamonds in – a pack of cards.

Love ceases to be a pleasure, when it ceases to be a secret.   (Aphra Behn)

Absence is to love what wind is to fire. It extinguishes the small, it kindles the great.

(Comte de Bussy-Rabutin)

His wife was a titled lady – she was the Southwest Light Heavyweight Champion.

Her husband's a hopeless gardener – he made a rock garden – and three rocks died.

A successful marriage involves falling in love many times – always with the same person.

I married beneath me. All women do. (Nancy Astor)

If you want to pull the wool over your husband's
eyes you need to have a good yarn.

My heart has made its mind up
And I'm afraid it's you. (Wendy Cope)

Happiness in marriage is entirely a matter of chance.
(Jane Austen)

I first saw her outside a pawnshop – she was
picking her teeth – so I went in the shop and helped
her pick the ones she wanted.

It is better to marry for purely selfish reasons.
(Anita Brookner)

'Births' column in paper: Baby flawless, mother
breathless, and father legless.

Mirrors are the perfect lovers. (Margaret Atwood)

I had an inheritance from my father,
It was the moon and sun,
And though I roam all over the world,
The spending of it's never done.

Husband comes home after visiting the doctor.
'The doctor said I have a hormone problem,
I need to have sex seven times a week.'
'OK love, you can put me down for a couple of
those.'

I admire the young, they have such strong
convictions. I saw a group of students the other day
with a big banner saying, 'Make love not war.'
I, of course, do both, I am married.

Her husband's not from Norway – but he does look
like a Norse.

Love is not only a feeling: it is also an art.

(Honoré de Balzac)

Married life requires shared mysteries even when all
the facts are known.   (Richard Ford)

'Egbert, Is it true married people live longer?'
'No, it just seems longer.'   (W C Fields)

13.
Management

He's got a very tasteful office. Nothing fancy – just a full length mirror and a throne.

I don't want any yes men in this team. I want people who speak their minds – even if it does cost them their jobs.

When I want your opinion I'll give it to you.

I asked her how many people worked in her department – she said, 'About half'.

Carve that on a tablet of stone and send it down the mountain.

The Receptionist at Head Office said, 'Have a nice day'. He said, 'Don't tell me what to do'.

If at first you don't succeed – your successor will.

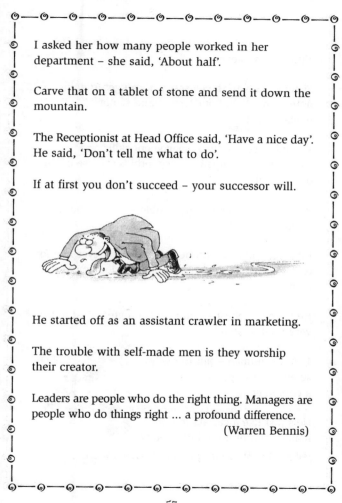

He started off as an assistant crawler in marketing.

The trouble with self-made men is they worship their creator.

Leaders are people who do the right thing. Managers are people who do things right ... a profound difference.

(Warren Bennis)

The only way he'll get to the top of the tree is by sitting on an acorn.

Fishing is about the closest you can get to doing nothing at all without getting into senior management.

We didn't see all his management skills and techniques – company policy forbids the use of cat o' nine tails.

Remember nothing is impossible – unless you have to do it yourself.

I have found some of the best reasons I ever had for remaining at the bottom – simply by looking at the men at the top.

He is very modest – and he's got a great deal to be very modest about.

To err is human – but to really screw things up you need a computer.

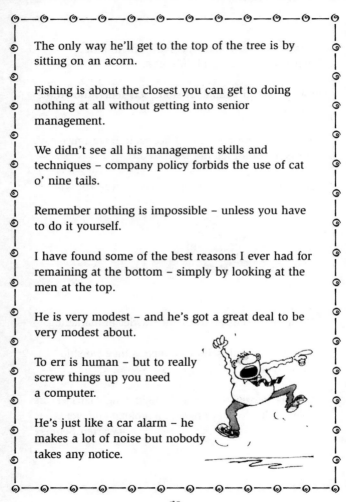

He's just like a car alarm – he makes a lot of noise but nobody takes any notice.

14.
Money Matters

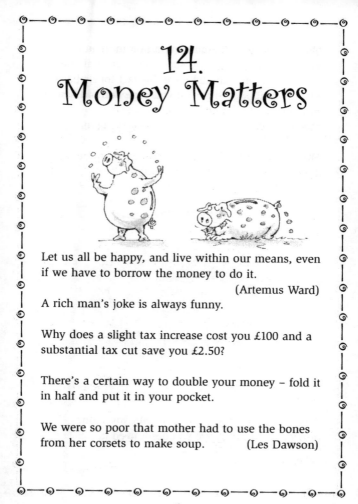

Let us all be happy, and live within our means, even if we have to borrow the money to do it.

(Artemus Ward)

A rich man's joke is always funny.

Why does a slight tax increase cost you £100 and a substantial tax cut save you £2.50?

There's a certain way to double your money – fold it in half and put it in your pocket.

We were so poor that mother had to use the bones from her corsets to make soup. (Les Dawson)

Money is indeed the most important thing in the world: and all sound and successful personal and national morality should have this fact for its basis.

(George Bernard Shaw)

Change is inevitable – except from vending machines.

There's lots of things more important than money – the only thing is they all *cost* money.

A banker is someone who will lend you money – provided you can prove you don't need it.

He started out with nothing – and he's still got most of it left.

When someone says 'It's the principle of the thing, not the money' – it's the money.

When somebody tell you that it's not a money problem, they're talking about somebody else's money.

(Bill Clinton)

Highwaymen demand your money or your life – women require both. (Samuel Butler)

A man has one hundred dollars and you leave him with two dollars, that's subtraction. (Mae West)

I wouldn't say it was a badly paid job but they offered a choice on paydays – fresh, roasted or salted.

I think crime pays. The hours are good, you travel a lot. (Woody Allen)

Debts are becoming for 25-year-olds; after this, no-one forgives them.

15.
Music

He was brought up in a musical environment – his family were all on the fiddle.

Music is life, and, like it, inextinguishable.

(Carl Nielson)

'Do you play requests?'
'Only when we're asked.'

Pianist – a disturber of the piano keys.

I'd give my right arm to be able to play the piano.

Each member of the band is a soloist in his own right. It's only when they play together they get into trouble.

All music is folk music. I ain't never heard no horse sing a song. (Louis Armstrong)

It was the kind of opera that started at eight o'clock and after you had been listening for three hours, your watch says eight twenty.

Opera is when a guy gets stabbed in the back and instead of dying he sings. (Robert Charles Benchley)

He doesn't know his aria from his elbow.

A saxophonist's definition of an optimist – a trombonist with an answering machine.

Extraordinary how potent cheap music is.
(Noel Coward)

I must confess that I live a miserable life ... I live entirely in my music.
(Beethoven)

'How is it you can play so well when you're pissed?' 'I practice when I'm pissed.'

Definition of a gentleman – someone who knows how to play the bagpipes – and doesn't.

They sound like a real band.
(Dizzy Gillespie)

His music is not so bad as it sounds.
(Mark Twain on Wagner)

I've seen better bands on a cigar.

His hi-fi's got more woofers than Battersea Dogs Home.

A drunk band is a happy band.

She got a flute for Christmas but she threw it away as it had holes in it.

He made a major contribution to the music world by staying out of it.

The music teacher came twice a week to try to bridge the awful gap between Dorothy and Chopin.

(George Ade)

Next song – it starts at the beginning, there's a bit in the middle, and then it peters out.

'I can make my clarinet talk.'
'What does it say – put me back in my case?'

Don't clap too hard – it's a very old building.

(John Osborne)

16.
People

Do not do unto others as you would they should do to you. Their tastes may not be the same.

(George Bernard Shaw)

Man is the only animal that blushes – or needs to.

(Mark Twain)

Some are wise – some are otherwise.

It is better to have loafed and lost than never loafed at all. (James Thurber)

I am free of all prejudice – I hate everyone equally.

(W C Fields)

I never forget a face – but in your case I'll make an exception. (Groucho Marx)

I have a fine sense of the ridiculous, but no sense of humour. (Edward Albee)

I don't have to look up my family tree, because I know I'm the sap. (Fred Allen)

Friendship is like a bank account – you can't continue to draw on it without making deposits.

All happy families resemble each other; each unhappy family is unhappy in its own way. (Leo Tolstoy)

If he'd only wash his neck, I'd wring it. (John Sparrow)

Politics brings you in contact with all the people you'd give anything to avoid.

They say one day he'll be Prime Minister – one day will be enough!

We shared a common interest – a mutual dislike of each other. (Jack Hawkins)

He's a man who can brighten up the whole room –
just by leaving it.

He's got both feet firmly planted in the air.

He has the personal presence
of Lord Lucan.

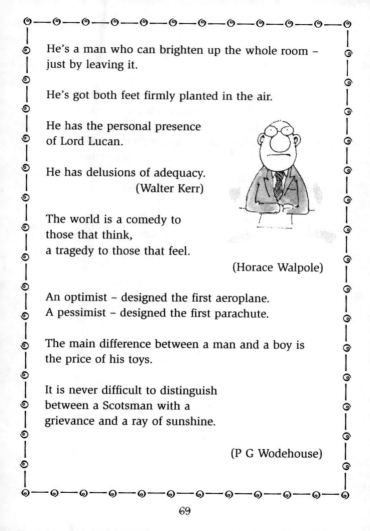

He has delusions of adequacy.
(Walter Kerr)

The world is a comedy to
those that think,
a tragedy to those that feel.

(Horace Walpole)

An optimist – designed the first aeroplane.
A pessimist – designed the first parachute.

The main difference between a man and a boy is
the price of his toys.

It is never difficult to distinguish
between a Scotsman with a
grievance and a ray of sunshine.

(P G Wodehouse)

He has a habit of finding things before they are actually lost.

Women are most fascinating between the ages of 35 and 40, after they have won a few races and know how to pace themselves. Since few women ever pass 40, maximum fascination can continue indefinitely.
(Christian Dior)

I hate to spread gossip – but what else can you do with it?

The person who doesn't gossip has no friends to speak of.

He's had the charisma bypass operation.

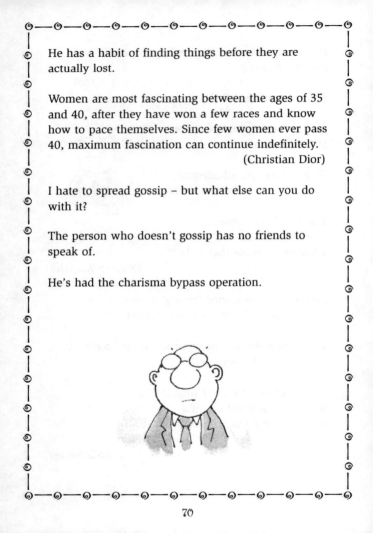

His family tree was full of nuts.

Animal lover: 'And there was one poor lion that didn't get a Christian.'

They were a tense and peculiar family the Oedipuses, weren't they. (Sir Max Beerbohm)

He'd kill for a Nobel Peace Prize.

Before you tell someone how good you are, you must tell them how bad you used to be.
(Semon Knudson)

People are not fallen angels. They are merely people.
(D H Lawrence)

17.
Profound Quotations

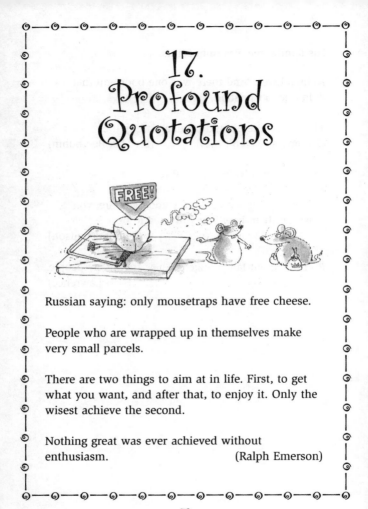

Russian saying: only mousetraps have free cheese.

People who are wrapped up in themselves make very small parcels.

There are two things to aim at in life. First, to get what you want, and after that, to enjoy it. Only the wisest achieve the second.

Nothing great was ever achieved without enthusiasm. (Ralph Emerson)

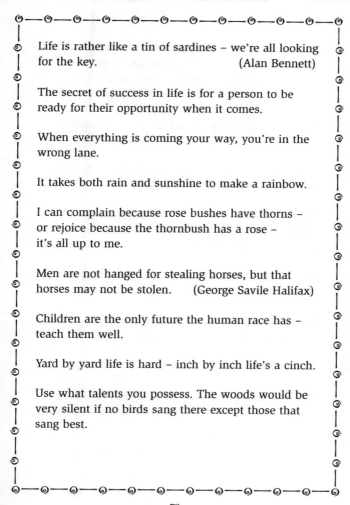

Life is rather like a tin of sardines – we're all looking
for the key.   (Alan Bennett)

The secret of success in life is for a person to be
ready for their opportunity when it comes.

When everything is coming your way, you're in the
wrong lane.

It takes both rain and sunshine to make a rainbow.

I can complain because rose bushes have thorns –
or rejoice because the thornbush has a rose –
it's all up to me.

Men are not hanged for stealing horses, but that
horses may not be stolen.   (George Savile Halifax)

Children are the only future the human race has –
teach them well.

Yard by yard life is hard – inch by inch life's a cinch.

Use what talents you possess. The woods would be
very silent if no birds sang there except those that
sang best.

My only solution for the problem of habitual accidents ... is to stay in bed all day. Even then, there is always the chance that you will fall out.
(Robert Benchley)

Do not fear the winds of adversity – remember a kite rises *against* the wind rather than with it.

The race is not always won by the swift – but often by those who keep on running.

Leaving reminds us of what we can part with and what we can't, then offers us something new to look forward to, to dream about.
(Richard Ford)

Some people dream of accomplishments while others stay awake and do them.

You cannot discover new oceans unless you have the courage to lose sight of the shore.

To be a winner all you need to give is all you have.

The art of conversation is knowing when to keep silent.
(Mark Twain)

Civilisation is a conspiracy.   (John Buchan)

Thinking is the hardest work there is, which is why
so few engage in it.   (Henry Ford)

The best manager is the one who has sense enough
to pick good men to do what he wants done and
self-restraint enough to keep from meddling with
them while they do it.   (Theodore Roosevelt)

You begin saving the world by saving one at a time;
all else is grandiose romanticism or politics.

Never play leapfrog with a unicorn.

It's the early bird that gets the worm, but it's the second mouse that gets the cheese.

Eagles may soar, but weasels don't get sucked into jet engines.

There's night and day, brother, both sweet things; sun, moon, and stars, brother, all sweet things; there's likewise a wind on the heath. Life is very sweet, brother; who would wish to die?

(George Borrow)

Never do today what you can put off till tomorrow.

The reason men are greater than animals isn't because we can dream of the stars ... it's because we have something they haven't. Greed.

(Harlan Ellison)

18.
Religion

A good life is the only religion.

God is subtle, but he
is not malicious.
(Albert Einstein)

God gave us two ears and
one mouth – so why don't
we listen twice as much
as we talk?

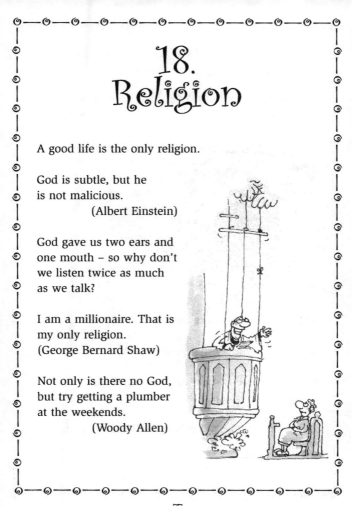

I am a millionaire. That is
my only religion.
(George Bernard Shaw)

Not only is there no God,
but try getting a plumber
at the weekends.
(Woody Allen)

19.
Sex

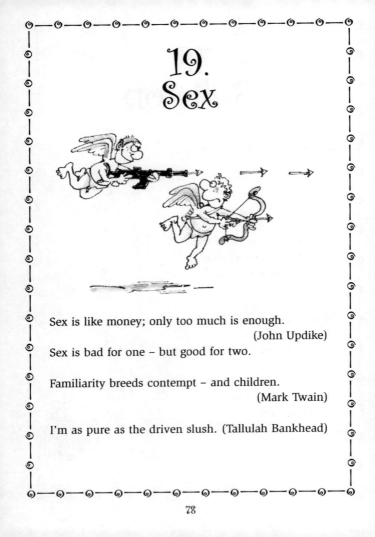

Sex is like money; only too much is enough.

(John Updike)

Sex is bad for one – but good for two.

Familiarity breeds contempt – and children.

(Mark Twain)

I'm as pure as the driven slush. (Tallulah Bankhead)

He's very good in bed – he goes straight to sleep.

Remember sex is not the answer. Sex is the question. Yes is the answer.

He got hold of this powdered rhino horn – it's a great aphrodisiac – the only trouble is he keeps charging Land Rovers.

His idea of a dirty weekend is cleaning out the coal shed.

Sex! What is that but life after all? We're all of us selling sex, because we're all selling life.

(Alvin Chereskin)

It doesn't matter what you do in the bedroom, as long as you don't do it in the street and frighten the horses.

(Mrs Patrick Campbell)

She used to be Snow White but she drifted.

(Mae West)

I'm no angel but I've spread my wings a bit.

(Mae West)

Let's forget about the six feet and talk about the seven inches.
(Mae West)

It's better to be looked over than overlooked.
(Mae West)

He said 'Come back to my place – I've got mirrors all over the walls and mirrors all over the ceiling – and bring a bottle.' So I went with a bottle of Windowlene.

She went back to his place and he asked 'Would you like super sex?'
'The way I'm feeling right now, could I just have the soup?'

If you cannot have your dear husband for a comfort and a delight, for a bread-winner and a crosspatch, for a sofa, chair or hot-water bottle, one can use him as a cross to be borne.
(Stevie Smith)

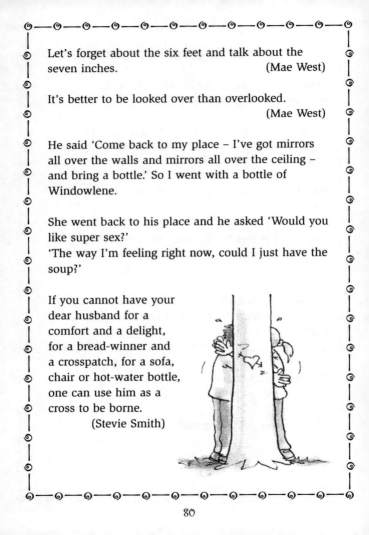

20. Smoking

You may smoke a cigar with abandon – but never with a band on.

Giving up smoking is easy – I've done it hundreds of times. (Mark Twain)

Giving up by using nicotine patches – you stick one over each eye and you can't find your fags.

I'm a father! I'm a father! Have a cigar.
Thanks – is it a boy or a girl?
I don't know – all cigars look the same to me.
(Groucho Marx)

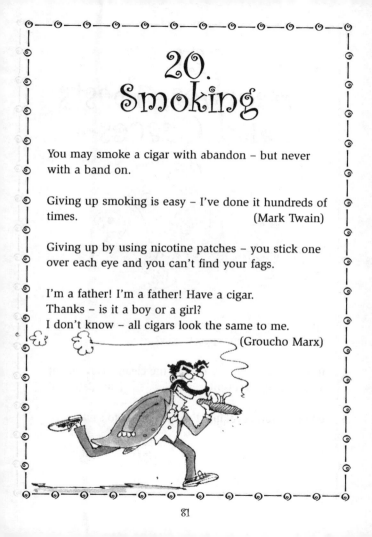

21.
Speeches, Toasts and Graces

Shall we let them enjoy themselves a bit longer or shall we have your speech now?

It is all too rare today to hear the clear, clean ring of a really original insult. (Jim Carrigan)

Before I start speaking, I've something to say.

I said I wouldn't have time to prepare a speech so I was told to say something off the top of my head – here's a short talk on dandruff.

Thank you! Of all the introductions I've heard over the years, that was the most (pause) recent.

Speak in French when you can't think of the English for a thing – turn out your toes as you walk – and remember who you are!
(Lewis Carroll, from *Through the Looking-Glass*)

It's a nice hotel this – lovely, fluffy towels – I could hardly get my case closed this morning.

I've had a wonderful evening –
but this wasn't it.
(Groucho Marx)

When you have
nothing to say,
say nothing.
(Charles Colton)

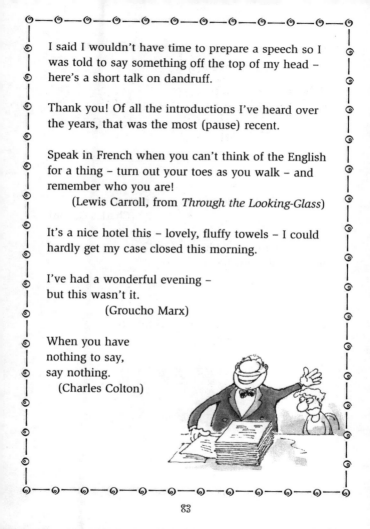

A verbal contract isn't worth the paper it's written on.

I'll give you a definite maybe.

Include me out.

We are dealing with facts not reality.

(Sam Goldwyn)

As the painter and decorator said, 'I'm overcome with emulsion.'

Imitation is the sincerest form of flattery.

(Charles Colton)

I thank you from the heart of my bottom – sorry, the bottom of my heart.

All generalisations are dangerous, even this one.
(Alexandre Dumas)

I was asked how I felt about toasting the guests and I was in favour of it – preferably over an open fire.

May you live as long as you want to, and want to as long as you live.

To wives/husbands and sweethearts.
May they never meet.

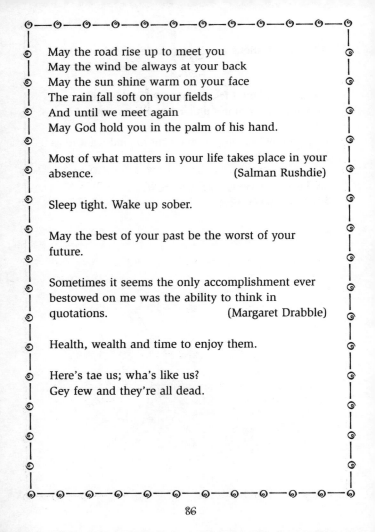

May the road rise up to meet you
May the wind be always at your back
May the sun shine warm on your face
The rain fall soft on your fields
And until we meet again
May God hold you in the palm of his hand.

Most of what matters in your life takes place in your absence.   (Salman Rushdie)

Sleep tight. Wake up sober.

May the best of your past be the worst of your future.

Sometimes it seems the only accomplishment ever bestowed on me was the ability to think in quotations.   (Margaret Drabble)

Health, wealth and time to enjoy them.

Here's tae us; wha's like us?
Gey few and they're all dead.

22.
Sport

I believe every human has a finite number of heartbeats. I don't intend to waste any of mine running around doing exercises. (Neil Armstrong)

Life's too short for chess. (Henry Byron)

Deer stalking would be a very fine sport if only the deer had guns. (W S Gilbert)

Rugby is a game played by men with peculiarly shaped balls.

Talking of rugby – do the Wasps have a 'B' team?

There are two things no man will admit he can't do well – drive and make love. (Stirling Moss)

Why is it that a fast bowler is allowed to strike a batsman on the head with the ball but the batsman can't hit the bowler on the head with his bat?

England have just chosen their team for the world cup – it's Brazil!

If he threw himself on the ground he'd miss.

The team's taking art lessons so they can draw bigger crowds.

The Club was asking for donations. I put a pound in an envelope and sent it in. Got a nice letter back from the Chairman thanking me and asking which two players I wanted.

Old football injury playing up again. I was watching 'Match of the Day' and I cut my thumb on a can of Carling Black Label.

Jogging is very beneficial. It's very good for your legs and feet. It's also good for the ground. It makes it feel needed.   (Charles Schultz)

Tennis is a game of no use in itself. (Francis Bacon)

All that I know surely about morality and the obligations of man, I owe to football.

(Albert Camus)

Golf

The secret of good golf is threefold – hit the ball hard, straight, and not too often.

I'm not saying he's is a bad golfer but he's been in more sand than Lawrence of Arabia.

'What's the longest ball you ever hit?'
'Three thousand miles – it went through the window of a plane.'

Golfer playing badly and blames caddy.
'You must be the worst caddy in the world.'
Caddy: 'No. That would be too much of a coincidence.'

This is a very hard course – how often do you see sand traps with headstones?

Golfer to pro: 'What do you think of my game?'
'Not bad, but I still prefer golf.'

A caddy was getting on the golfer's nerves 'Are you anxious to get home or what? Every time I hit the ball you look at your watch.'
'It's not a watch, it's a compass.'

A golfer getting fed up with opponents' constant chattering hits the ball into a bunker.
Opponent: 'There's an even worse trap than that on this course.'
'I know, why don't you shut it?'

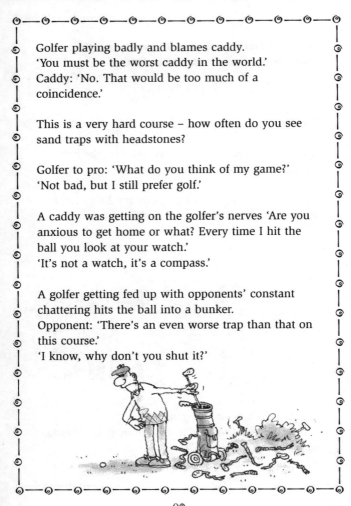

90

23.
Travel

'A return ticket please.'

'Where to?'

'Here, of course.'   (Tommy Cooper)

The next train has gone ten minutes ago.

The trouble with America is that there are far too many wide open spaces surrounded by teeth.
                                       (Charles Luckman)

California is a fine place to live in – if you happen to be an orange.   (Fred Allen)

Two lions walking down the High Street in Torquay – 'Not very busy here, is it?'

'I'm from London.'

'What part?'

'All of me.'

Cockney just off the boat in Jersey.
''Ere mate, where's the nearest boozer?'
Resident: 'You're looking at him.'

'Have you lived here all your life?'
'Not yet.'

Car sticker – Alfa Romeo is better than none.

Ramparts – only of interest to sheep.

SAGA Holidays – Send A Granny Away.

The forecast is getting better – God knows what the *weather* is going to do.

To journey is better than to arrive – or so say those who have already arrived. (Fay Weldon)

It wasn't the fall that killed him – it was the sudden stop when he hit the ground.

A climber, lost in the mist, smells what seem to be fish and chips. He then sees a Monastery ahead with a couple of priests at the entrance.
'You must be the Friar.'
'No, he's the frier. I'm the chip monk.'

My experience of ships is that on them one makes an interesting discovery about the world. One finds one can do without it completely.
(Malcolm Stanley Bradbury)

24.
Unlucky

If his boat came in he'd be waiting at the airport.

Pessimist – never happy unless he's miserable.

Living in the lap of luxury – then it stood up.

They called him Vic because he got up everyone's nose.

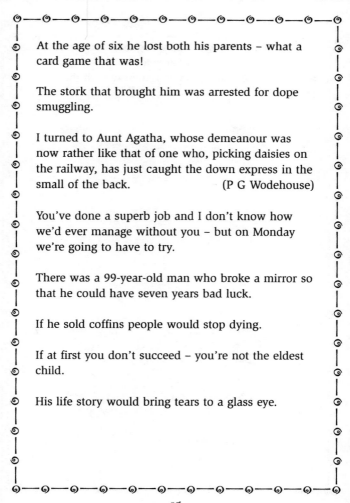

At the age of six he lost both his parents – what a card game that was!

The stork that brought him was arrested for dope smuggling.

I turned to Aunt Agatha, whose demeanour was now rather like that of one who, picking daisies on the railway, has just caught the down express in the small of the back.　(P G Wodehouse)

You've done a superb job and I don't know how we'd ever manage without you – but on Monday we're going to have to try.

There was a 99-year-old man who broke a mirror so that he could have seven years bad luck.

If he sold coffins people would stop dying.

If at first you don't succeed – you're not the eldest child.

His life story would bring tears to a glass eye.

He had this friend who had a dog that was a cross between a Pit Bull and a Labrador puppy – it scared the shit out of him, and then ran away with the toilet roll.

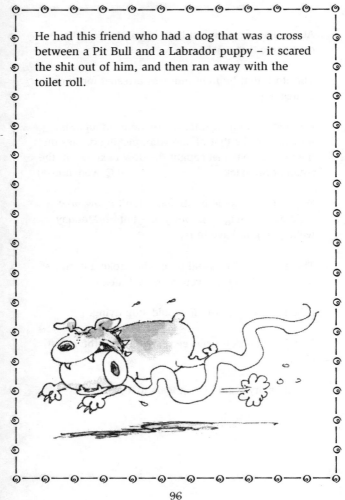